A romance of the Asiatic invasion of Australia

THE YELLOW WAVE

JANE MILLER

From the novel by
Kenneth Mackay

Currency Press,
Sydney

CURRENT THEATRE SERIES

First published in 2017
by Currency Press Pty Ltd,
PO Box 2287, Strawberry Hills, NSW, 2012, Australia
enquiries@currency.com.au
www.currency.com.au

in association with La Mama Theatre, Melbourne

Cataloguing-in-publication data for this title is available from the National Library of Australia website: www.nla.gov.au

Typeset by Dean Nottle for Currency Press.
Printed by Fineline Print + Copy Services, St Peters, NSW
Cover design: Karen Slade (Brief Eater Design) and Katy Wall.
Photography: Pier Carthew.
Cover image shows Keith Brockett and John Marc Desengano.
La Mama Schools Publication Coordinator: Maureen Hartley.

Contents

ACKNOWLEDGEMENTS

Thank you to the following people for their generous contribution of time, resources and artistry to the development of *The Yellow Wave*:

Christie Nieman, Miki Brotzler, Zachary Ruane, Tania Lentini, The Poppy Seed Festival, Theatreworks and The Butterfly Club.

The Yellow Wave was first produced as part of the Poppy Seed Festival at the Butterfly Club, Melbourne, on 17 November 2015, with the following cast:

PERFORMER	Keith Brockett
PERFORMER	John Marc Desengano
NARRATOR	Andrea McCannon

Director, Beng Oh
Designer, Emily Collett
Lighting Designer, Matthew Barber

CHARACTERS

NARRATOR
PHILIP ORLOFF
COUNT ZENSKI
HEATHER CAMERON
HARDEN, hypnotist
SIR ANGUS CAMERON
DICK HATTEN
TED JOHNSON
EDITH ENSON
MRS ENSON
SIR ROBERT, NSW Premier
MINISTER OF WAR
ALEXIS DROMEROFF
BILLY
IO
OLD MARGARET
SIR PETER MCLOSKIE, Queensland Premier
MR MUSGRAVE
MESSENGER
GENERAL LEROY
COMMISSIONER WANG
KALMUCK SOLIDER 1
KALMUCK SOLDIER 2

SETTING

Australia, 1885 and now.

Centre stage, there is a bench. To one side of it is a gong and on the walls around, propaganda posters warning of 'Asian Invasion'.

This play went to press before the end of rehearsals and may differ from the play as performed.

NARRATOR: Sometimes a book is more than a book.

Sometimes it's a window through which we can see an unexplored horizon.

The Yellow Wave is just such a book. Set in the nineteenth century and subtitled 'A romance of the Asiatic invasion of Australia', it is a story with everything. There is literally nothing it doesn't have.

Featuring a cast of heroic characters, *The Yellow Wave* introduces us first to swarthy-cheeked, hot-tempered former soldier, Philip Orloff, and enigmatic, urbane Russian rail builder, Count Zenski. Later, we also meet salt-of-the-earth renaissance man of the land, Dick Hatten.

In the heart of this classic work of literature beats a love story bigger than the country in which it is set. *The Yellow Wave* recounts the passionate love of Philip Orloff and Dick Hatten for one extraordinary woman.

That woman is Heather Cameron. Heather Cameron, the kind of heroine found in the work of Austen and Brontë. Heather Cameron, a woman pale of both skin and personality.

Our story begins in 1885 aboard a magnificent cruise liner as it makes its way across the Arabian Sea, bound for Australia. On board, the ship's passengers sail blissfully unaware that in the distance an alien force is planning the invasion of an innocent young continent at the bottom of the world.

Action sequence: Mongol force indicating they are making plans.

NARRATOR: It is on the deck of the ship, the *SS Genoa*, following an evening of wining, dining and dancing, that we first meet the suave, sophisticated Count Zenski.

ZENSKI: How dull these English are! So merciless to anyone or anything foreign, so partial to all things English. *Peste*, they are *bourgeois* at heart, every one, utterly ignorant of everything.

ORLOFF *enters.*

ORLOFF: Count Zenski.

ZENSKI: Philip Orloff.

ORLOFF: Do you believe in hypnotism, Count Zenski?

ZENSKI: Interesting question, *mon ami.*

ORLOFF: Do you remember the other night when that fellow Harden tested his willpower on some of the passengers?

ZENSKI: Harden? He has the receding chin and facial features of womanlike delicacy. No?

ORLOFF: That's him.

ZENSKI: I seem to recall his greatest success was with one Miss Heather Cameron?

ORLOFF: Since then he has seemed to exert a strange fascination over her.

ZENSKI: Please explain.

ORLOFF: A few minutes ago, I asked Miss Cameron to dance … dance … dance … Miss Cameron, if I'm not mistaken, the next dance is ours.

HEATHER: Alright, Philip.

ORLOFF: I felt her delicate touch on my arm and then from nowhere that devil Harden appears.

HARDEN: Miss Cameron. I believe this is our dance. Am I not right? Miss Cameron. Come, dance with me.

HEATHER: I'm sorry, Philip. You have made a mistake.

ORLOFF: Nonsense, Miss Cameron! I assure you, I am quite right.

HARDEN: Miss Cameron? Dance with me.

HEATHER: Yes, Mr Harden. I'll dance with you.

ORLOFF: Damn that devil!

HEATHER *exits with* HARDEN, *ignoring* ORLOFF.

Well, what do you say to that, Zenski?

ZENSKI: I say that if a woman wants to go to the devil, never interfere. If she prefers Harden, why not?

ORLOFF: A thousand reasons.

ZENSKI: Come now, Philip, turn your mind elsewhere.

Asia lies as a rich and boundless field for the servants of the Czar.

ORLOFF: Asia? What's Asia got to do with anything?

ZENSKI: It has a lot to offer for a man of ambition.

If you take my meaning?

ORLOFF: What do you mean?

ZENSKI: You are young, strong, and a soldier.

I merely point out a direction in which you will find scope for your ambition. Understand me, *mon ami?*

ORLOFF: Do you mean I should go to Asia?

ZENSKI: I have friends. Do you picture the splendid portrait of the future I am painting?

ORLOFF: You want me to go to Asia with your friends? Are they Russian?

ZENSKI: No, listen … I am saying … I have friends with power. Friends with power. Now, do you see what I am suggesting?

NARRATOR: Just what Count Zenski is suggesting is no clearer the next morning.

ZENSKI: Powerful friends. See what I am saying?

ORLOFF: When you say Asia … do you mean China? You want me to go to China? Is it a holiday? What's the weather like?

NARRATOR: That evening we meet Sir Angus Cameron, father of Heather.

CAMERON: Hurry along, Count. You know whist waits for no man.

ZENSKI: Ah, Sir Angus, our rubber! These card players are inexorable.

NARRATOR: Cameron and Zenski's departure paves the way for the most ardent of exchanges.

ORLOFF: A penny for your thoughts, Heather.

HEATHER: —

ORLOFF: Where have you been hiding all day?

HEATHER: I have been lying down.

ORLOFF: You look half asleep now!

HEATHER: Do I? I always seem tired here. I wish we were in Sydney.

ORLOFF: Heather, treat me as a dog if you will, but not like a fool!

HEATHER: I won't be treated like a schoolgirl, Philip.

ORLOFF: Why did you give Harden my dance and leave me standing like a fool? Without even one word of explanation?

HEATHER: Whatever are you talking about?

ORLOFF: Do you mean you don't remember?

HEATHER: How can you expect me to remember what never happened?

ORLOFF: Has this man hypnotised you? Like he did that night in the saloon? Think, Heather, for God's sake!

HEATHER: No, Philip.

ORLOFF: Promise me that you won't ever allow him.

HEATHER: Of course I won't, Philip, if you don't wish it.

ORLOFF: I only wish one thing.

HEATHER: Yes, Philip.

ORLOFF *drops to one knee.*

ORLOFF: My darling Heather. I love none but you, my precious girl. Marry me.

HEATHER: —

ORLOFF: Darling, your answer! You love me; why hesitate?

HEATHER: —

ORLOFF: For God's sake, Heather. Don't say I deceived myself!

HARDEN *enters.* HEATHER *rises, waves* ORLOFF *aside, moves quickly past him and stands next to* HARDEN.

HARDEN: You love me, Heather? Don't you? You love me?

HEATHER: I love you, Mr Harden.

ORLOFF: Heather, this is insane!

HARDEN: Now come with me, Miss Heather … where we can be alone. Alone. Do you understand?

HEATHER: Yes. Alone.

CAMERON *and* ZENSKI *enter.*

CAMERON: Och … I have been looking everywhere for you, Heather.

HARDEN: I fear I am to blame. We were just passing the time, weren't we, Miss Cameron? Just passing time.

HEATHER: Yes … passing time.

CAMERON: Och, I don't suppose any harm's done. Come on then, Heather. Night, all.

CAMERON, HEATHER *and* HARDEN *exit.*

ZENSKI: You are bad company tonight, Philip. Is it an affair of the liver or the heart?

ORLOFF: Tonight I again saw this man exert his strange power. Damn him, with his receding chin and features of woman-like delicacy.

ZENSKI: In what manner?

ORLOFF: Tonight I asked Heather to marry me.

ZENSKI: *Mon Dieu!*

ORLOFF: By the light in her eyes, I knew she was mine. Then, as her lips moved, they became cold. It was Harden. 'You love me', the devil said; and she replied as one repeating a lesson, 'I love you'. She has no memory of the spells this man casts over her.

ZENSKI: Philip, believe one who has known many, many, many women, seen the sordidness of their passions and betrayals; they are not worth it.

ORLOFF: Zenski, I can't let this girl go out of my life. Her love has become part of my being.

ZENSKI: Remember, Philip, a successful soldier saves all his worship for the shrine of ambition.

ORLOFF: What does that mean?

ZENSKI: Our conversation? My friends? Broadening your horizons?

ORLOFF: What? Look, I told you before, Zenski, I'm not interested in that Chinese trip with your Russian friends.

NARRATOR: With that, Orloff bids Zenski goodnight, leaving us to wonder at the vague inferences about Russian chums and broad horizons.

There are more than inferences in store the next day as matters come to a head in Harden's cabin.

ORLOFF: Do you intend to marry Miss Cameron?

HARDEN: Don't be absurd, Orloff! If the girl prefers me, surely that is her affair; you heard what she said last night.

ORLOFF: You forced her to say it.

HARDEN: My dear fellow, what humbug! She happens to prefer me to you—devilish bad taste on her part.

ORLOFF: Do you mean to make her your wife?

HARDEN: A fellow must do something to amuse himself on board ship.

ORLOFF: You shuffling cur! How dare you force her to say she loved you unless you meant to marry her?!

HARDEN: Marry her? You jealous fool!

ORLOFF: Are you prepared to marry Heather Cameron? By God, I will have an answer.

HARDEN: Curse you! I mean to amuse myself with her till she bores me. Then you can have her, and welcome.

ORLOFF: You hound.

HARDEN *starts to hypnotise* ORLOFF.

HARDEN: Listen to me, Philip Orloff. Listen to my voice. Hear me. Follow my finger. I will do as I please with Miss Heather Cameron. She is a play thing. A trifle. Mine to do with as I please. Understand, Orloff? Hear me. Follow? Now sit. Stay. Drop. Roll over.

ORLOFF *falls momentarily under his spell and shakes it off.*

ORLOFF: You foul dog.

ORLOFF *stabs* HARDEN *in the heart.*

HARDEN: Why …?

HARDEN *falls to the ground, dead.* ZENSKI *enters.*

ZENSKI: Ah, Monsieur Harden! Poor devil! With his receding chin and features of woman-like delicacy, not to mention that dagger in his heart.

ORLOFF: He tried his damn tricks and I stabbed him.

ORLOFF *throws the dagger aside.*

ZENSKI: Philip, I would like to have a little chat with you. May I smoke?

ORLOFF: Zenski! How can you talk of chatting here?

ZENSKI: Why not? Harden will be discreet. Why you killed him I do not know, but the authorities will hang you.

ORLOFF: I am prepared to accept the consequences.

ZENSKI: Time is short—I will save you from yourself. You are too useful to dangle from the end of a rope.

ORLOFF: It's not ideal, but it has to be faced.

ZENSKI: Not so. Lend me your ear.

ZENSKI *whispers in a language we assume may be Russian. The* NARRATOR *stands on the other side of* ORLOFF *and interprets.*

NARRATOR: If Orloff agrees to this and pledges his honour to the czar, he can escape.

ORLOFF: Escape!

NARRATOR: A Russian warship will be waiting for him in the bay. If he serves the czar, he will have nothing to worry about in the East.

ORLOFF: The East? Zenski, is that about the Chinese trip again and those Russian friends of yours?

ZENSKI: What is your answer?

One word will set in motion your escape, *mon ami.* You will be free as the breeze.

NARRATOR: Wind.

ZENSKI: Free as the wind.

ORLOFF: Alright, I'll do it.

I'll entertain your damn Russian friends … But I am telling you this, Zenski. I won't wear a kaftan and I don't know how to use chopsticks. But I'm prepared to learn.

ZENSKI: Then we have a deal, *mon ami.*

They shake.

NARRATOR: The next morning the ship docks for a stopover in Colombo, carrying one less passenger, and with Philip Orloff confined a prisoner to his cabin.

Or is he?

CAMERON: Damned seedy business, Count. I don't want my Heather anywhere near that Orloff. Lucky he showed his true colours before it went too far.

ZENSKI: Not so lucky for friend Harden, *eh, mon ami*?

CAMERON: What baffles me is where he's got to. Damned scoundrel's vanished.

ZENSKI: Into the slim air.

NARRATOR: Thin.

CAMERON: But, Zenski, where do you think that ruffian Orloff has gone?

ZENSKI: To the devil, *mon ami*. To the devil.

NARRATOR: Thus, *The Yellow Wave* concludes its time on the high seas with a crime of passion, a thrilling escape and a mysterious bargain between Zenski and Orloff.

Not one to let the grass grow, our author moves the action forward nine years to the wide, brown Land Down Under.

It is in the rainswept streets of Sydney, during the horseracing season, that we first meet Dick Hatten. Dick Hatten, owner of a small cattle run and mare called Io.

Dick Hatten, part-time jockey, full-time Renaissance man. Dick Hatten, a man whose unrequited passion for Heather Cameron, as she pines for the fugitive Philip Orloff, is as awe-inspiring as his enduring friendship with tough, trustworthy, sun-tanned, Ted Johnson.

TED: Putting another five hundred on, Dick? Word is, Io can't miss.

DICK: That's just the devil of it, Ted. If this rain keeps on it's anybody's race.

TED: She's fit, and likes mud.

DICK: That's right enough, Ted, but how long are they going to ask me to keep her fit?

TED: About three weeks, from the look of this rain.

NARRATOR: Horses are very much on the mind of the women as *The Yellow Wave* introduces the complicated sexual politics of the period through the eyes of Heather, her friend Edith, and Edith's mother, Mrs Enson.

EDITH: Oh, Heather, this awful rain, my dream of a frock is born to blush unseen in that stupid stand.

HEATHER: Ted will still admire it, Edith.

EDITH: Ted indeed! Why, his tastes don't rise higher than a horsecloth!

MRS ENSON: I am surprised at you, Edith! Ted is prouder of you than you deserve.

EDITH: Mother … the only chance I'd have of Ted expressing pride is if I were a jockey.

HEATHER: You're a little plump for a jockey, Edith.

EDITH: What the dickens!

MRS ENSON: Heather!

EDITH: You're as bad as Ted. He says if I were a horse I'd want steady exercise every morning—the brute!

MRS ENSON: Isn't it time those young men were back?

EDITH: Oh, they won't hurry. We're not worth a thought when horses are under discussion.

HEATHER: I do love a good horse myself.

EDITH: Well, I hope Io wins. Ted told me that Dick has put every penny he has in the world on her.

NARRATOR: The Sydney race crowd is shocked by news of the invasion of India by Russia. Rumour runs rife as to what Russia is planning and whether Australia will be next. It is at an elegant cocktail *soirée* at the Midas Club that we find Dick, somewhat a fish out of water, chewing over these very matters with the New South Wales Premier and a government minister.

SIR ROBERT: It's as clear as day. Russian officers direct the advance and in no time the czar will pour one hundred thousand men through the gates of India. Isn't that right, Hatten?

DICK: Perhaps not one hundred thousand—

MINISTER OF WAR: My dear sir, you are as bad as these alarmists who have been attempting to scare England into hysterical action.

SIR ROBERT: I just cannot imagine why the mother country won't act on Russia. What do you say, Hatten?

DICK: Russia is powerful in the East—

MINISTER OF WAR: Russia's power in the East is exaggerated; England will assert herself when necessary.

ZENSKI *enters unseen by the others.*

DICK: That might be sooner than we think—

ZENSKI *steps forward.* DICK *is startled.*

Count.

ZENSKI: Dick Hatten, Sir Robert … I see we share a passion for the charms of the Sydney social *milieu.* Allow me to introduce you both to my friend Mr Alexis Dromeroff.

DROMEROFF *bows to* SIR ROBERT *and* DICK.

DROMEROFF: Hello.

ZENSKI: My friend has just come from Russia. He finds it better to remain at a distance from our great White Father.

DROMEROFF: Living under British laws, you know little of what life in Russia means for a man who dares to think for himself.

ZENSKI: Alexis was lucky not find himself headed directly to Siberia.

DROMEROFF: Thank goodness my old friend's letter came telling me of this grand new land of yours. So here I am.

DICK: You a revolutionary type, Mr Dromeroff?

DROMEROFF: Not at all. Dick Hat-ten.

SIR ROBERT: We are ready to welcome any and all Russians who help build a nation. Count Zenski has shown what you Russians can do up north.

ZENSKI: Bah! It is nothing. I have built you a few railway lines, laid a few simple tracks for your cha-cha trains.

NARRATOR: Choo-choo.

ZENSKI: Your choo-choo trains.

SIR ROBERT: But what do you think about this Russian invasion of India? Is Australia next?

DROMEROFF: *Mes amis*, Russia would love nothing more than to get its hands on Australia's rich possessions, but I cannot imagine she is planning to enter your beautiful country uninvited, just yet.

NARRATOR: It's all very convivial, but are Zenski and Dromeroff all they seem?

Amid all the talk of possible invasion, the book takes a moment to appreciate the quintessentially colourful characters of the Land Down Under and their love of the punt.

DICK: She looks pink, Billy.

BILLY: My oath!

DICK: On her feed?

BILLY: She's never off it.

DICK: I must win tomorrow, Billy.

BILLY: My oath.

DICK: But do you think I can? If the mare goes down, every penny I have goes with her.

BILLY: Gor bloom me! Look here, Mister Dick, d'ye remember that day on the Flinders when you met me with Matilda up, pig-jumping over them blooming sandhills, leading my blooming mater-bag?

DICK: When you were on the wallaby, you mean?

BILLY: Yes, per boot. Well, you gave me a lift on the packhorse and a pull at your flask, and we ain't parted since, have we?

DICK: No, Billy. We haven't. Come on, mate.

NARRATOR: There's more love to come in the form of Renaissance man Dick Hatten's eternally unrequited passion for pale Heather Cameron.

DICK: Heather …

HEATHER: You startled me out of a daydream, Dick.

DICK: And I was not the prince you expected, I fear.

HEATHER: He only comes in dreams.

But I do hope for your sake Io will win.

DICK: Then you do take a little interest in me?

HEATHER: I know all you have risked on the race. Everyone in old Banana Land is behind you. As your friend, I wish you success from the bottom of my heart.

DICK: Heather, can we never be something more?

All my life has been an aimless wandering.

I have been a sailor without a star. Now you have come into my life, I feel that there is a future to live for.

HEATHER: I know you will hate me for talking like this.

I cannot love you, Dick. But let us be friends.

DICK: For the present I accept your offer to be my own familiar friend.

HEATHER *sighs and stares blankly into the distance.*

Heather? What are you looking at?

HEATHER: My eye ventures to an impossible horizon.

Searching for he that is far beyond the reach of hand or eye, but closer to my heart than ever.

NARRATOR: Meanwhile, little do Heather and Dick realise that right under their noses some horizons are becoming increasingly less distant.

Action sequence: Invaders getting closer.

NARRATOR: For now, what the characters don't know won't hurt them. It's race day and there is nothing more stirring than Australia's love affair with the dignified sport of kings.

As the big race commences, the eager crowd anxiously await the crack of the starter's gun.

Action sequence: Grand National horse race.

NARRATOR: Io comes out strongly and takes a credible lead with Sardius second and Satan in third. Hang on … what's this? Sardius is down. She's down! She's taken Io with her. Io is down. Satan gallops on but this is a tragedy, punters. Two horses down … two down … But wait … Io is back up. She's back up. On her feet. It's a miracle. Credit Dick Hatten. What a rider. What a horse. Io is catching Satan on the home straight. As we near the finish, it's Io, it's Io. Io wins. Io wins the Grand National.

Hang on … this is strange! Heather Cameron has just appeared on the track. And she's tossing flowers … tossing them to Dick Hatten … Drop those blooms, man, drop them … Well, I hope those flowers smell very sweet because they spell instant disqualification for Dick Hatten and Io. What a day of mixed fortunes for the mare and her rider. All for a bunch of flowers.

DICK: Flowers! I can't fathom it, Ted.

TED: A simple mistake. A simple woman's mistake.

DICK: Not so simple.

TED: I didn't think Heather was such a fool.

DICK: Neither did I, but never mind.

TED: What about the Russians collaring India? Old Zenski said something about our sending a contingent of men over. You going?

DICK: I gave that up years ago. The last time I saw action was in Orloff's Mounted Rifles in Brisbane.

TED: Orloff? Philip Orloff? Isn't he that chap who stabbed the fellow on the ship, nine years back?

DICK: That's him. Orloff was a hot-tempered fellow, but straight as they come.

TED: I wonder what became of him after that boat business?

DICK: In any case, Ted, I fancy we'll need an army at home before long.

TED: Why?

DICK: Invasion. Queensland is full of Russians and cheap Chinese labour. I just don't cotton to these oily foreigners.

TED: I don't like them either, Dick, but you know what a devil of a time the unions gave us before they let in the cheap Chinese labour.

DICK: Old Zenski and his crowd will give us a worse time than any union. I don't trust that sneering old devil as far as I can pitch him.

NARRATOR: As Dick begins to suspect the motives of Russian rail barons, Zenski and Dromeroff, everyone is worried about the threat of invasion to Australia. Amidst the turmoil, we find the Queensland Premier and Count Zenski discussing the merit of cheap Chinese labour.

SIR PETER: This cheap Chinese labour has a lot of merit, Zenski. Trade is flourishing, and the unions are ruined.

ZENSKI: The land certainly thrives in the hands of the cheap Chinese labour.

SIR PETER: As long as this cheap Chinese labour doesn't turn on us, Zenski.

ZENSKI: Bah! Mr Premier, these Chinamen are slaves. A crack of the whip will always frighten beasts of burden.

NARRATOR: Slaves indeed, just as Dick's heart is to the charms of Heather.

HEATHER: What is it, Dick?

DICK: Heather, am I still to drift on like one of those goalless atoms—one of a great company, and still alone?

HEATHER: Dick, I too am searching for my star; will you bear me company?

DICK: Heather, I have found my star; and even if in searching for yours I lose it forever, I will bear you company.

HEATHER: Oh, Dick.

NARRATOR: Yes, passion doesn't come much grander, but it's time to farewell the Sydney slice of this monumental narrative. The Viceroy of India has requested five thousand Australian troops to help secure its borders from further invasion.

VICEROY: Get me some Australians!

NARRATOR: Unfortunately, Dick's race disqualification brings about his financial ruin as the mortgage on his cattle station is foreclosed.

DICK: I'm ruined. Financially.

NARRATOR: On the train trip back to Queensland two old friends toast their future plans.

ZENSKI: Five … five thousand Australian men to India. We have the train lines at our disposal while this contingent leaves us to our own devices. We are certainly in an enviable position, *mon ami.*

DROMEROFF: Outwardly our army is meant for India, but a Chinese fleet is ready to throw thirty … thirty thousand men on Australia.

ZENSKI: Thirty thousand Chinese will take this country.

DROMEROFF: Australia is to be had for the taking. Will you be ready for us?

ZENSKI: The way is clear. Cattle, horses even sheep are to be got everywhere in this land of plenty.

DROMEROFF: Australia will be ours. With a little help from our Chinese friends.

ZENSKI: Fill your glass, Dromeroff.

DROMEROFF: To the Yellow Wave!

ZENSKI: To the Yellow Wave!

ZENSKI *and* DROMEROFF *laugh sinister laughs.*

NARRATOR: On that sinister note, events leap forward three months, and we travel to God's own country. Queensland. The home of the cane toad. The tropical heart of Australia.

Following the events in Sydney, most of the characters, even some whose names we can't remember, head to Isis Downs, a large cattle station located in the land of the golden pineapple.

Meanwhile Dick, horse disqualified, homestead repossessed and heart still pining for Heather, has been roaming the countryside licking his wounds.

Until now! Dick suddenly appears at Isis Downs and happens upon a local chicken and turkey herder as she goes about her daily chores.

MARGARET: Get away there, old McFee. You leave Aunty Fanny alone, Frampton. Collins, get down, I say.

DICK: Hullo, Maggie!

MARGARET: Augh, glory be to God, if it isn't Mister Dick, with a beard on him like a billy goat!

DICK: Draw it mild, Maggie. How are they all up at the house?

MARGARET: Augh, fine, Mister Dick. God be praised, the spotted pig had the most beautiful litter you ever clapped eyes on.

DICK: And Miss Heather?

MARGARET: Augh, now, Mister Dick, wouldn't you like to ask her your own sweet self?

HEATHER *enters.*

HEATHER: Oh, Dick. I'm so glad you have come back.

DICK: Are you, Heather?

DICK *runs his hand over Io's mane.*

HEATHER: I've been riding Io every morning lately. Oh look, here's Billy.

BILLY *enters, bridle in arm.*

BILLY: Got back, I see, boss.

DICK: I'm just glad to see that Io is alright.

BILLY: Miss Heather's been riding her regular. Doing a fine job, she is.

HEATHER: Then you'd give me a mount, Billy?

BILLY: Blow me if I wouldn't! Your hands is light, and you sit square.

HEATHER: You've missed a lot around here, Dick. I detest gossip, but Edith's mother is very taken with Count Zenski.

DICK: Really? In future, it might be handy to be able to claim a connection to the count.

HEATHER: What do you mean? I detest mysteries.

DICK: Count Zenski is, if I am not vastly mistaken, a Russian spy.

HEATHER: Dick, I thought you were above the old English prejudice against foreigners.

DICK: Since five thousand of our best men have gone to India, there's nothing to stop Russia, using Zenski's rail lines, to waltz right into the heart of Queensland.

HEATHER: Oh, Dick! And what then?

DICK: A fight against terrible odds against a horde of bloodthirsty savages.

HEATHER: Savages?

DICK: Chinese.

HEATHER: Chinese!?

DICK: Chinese savages.

HEATHER: Chinese savages!

Oh, Dick!

Well, Mr Musgrave must have the same ideas. He has been putting Fort Mallarraway in a state of defence.

DICK: Musgrave is no fool. God help us if he alone is wise.

HEATHER: Oh, Dick!

NARRATOR: Oh, Dick indeed! And who is this Mr Musgrave with his lone wisdom and head full of ideas?

For now, there is some brief respite from unrest while the novel turns its attention to the love men bear each other and good old Aussie mateship.

TED: Well, what the devil do you want?

DICK: A little civility, or, if you can't supply that, five minutes on the grass.

TED: Dick, old man, I didn't know you with that confounded stubble! Put it there, if it weighed a ton!

DICK *and* TED *shake hands.*

We heard of your misfortune.

DICK: I have nothing left but Io and the two stockhorses.

TED: You've been as close to bottom before today.

DICK: Yes, but Queensland wasn't a slave province then. I think I'll cut it.

TED: Lots of time to think about that when we're tired of you, Dick.

NARRATOR: Ted may not be tired of Dick but he's getting pretty weary of Edith Enson's interest in Count Zenski's offsider, the shadowy Alexis Dromeroff.

EDITH: Talking of Russians, I wonder if we will ever see that delightful Mr Dromeroff again—he was so amusing.

TED: I for one couldn't care if we never saw Dromeroff again.

EDITH: Ted, are you jealous? Why shouldn't I like him if I wish?

TED: I detest foreigners.

EDITH: Well, on the whole I agree with you, so let us make it up.

NARRATOR: What a complex picture *The Yellow Wave* paints of the inner workings of relationships!

Meanwhile, more talk of the Mr Musgrave and his fortifications over a dinner at Isis Downs with Heather, Ted, Dick and Sir Angus.

CAMERON: What's the news with Musgrave?

TED: He's been making his place a fortress.

CAMERON: Poor old chap, he's mad, sure enough!

TED: If Musgrave's mad then so am I.

DICK: Musgrave and the Mallarraway people are the only ones who understand the danger.

HEATHER: What danger is that, Dick?

DICK: Five thousand of our best men have sailed for India.

HEATHER: On a boat, Dick?

DICK: Russia has attacked India. Australia could be next.

TED: You don't mean an invasion, Dick?

DICK: An invasion, Ted.

HEATHER: An invasion, Dick?

DICK: An invasion, Heather.

HEATHER: On a boat, Dick?

CAMERON: Och, an invasion, Dick! You're joking, man!

TED: If Dick's joking, then so am I.

CAMERON: Och. In any case … it would be an attack on our capitals.

HEATHER: I don't like the sound of an attack on our capitals.

DICK: The whole of Queensland is in the hands of foreigners. Who do you suppose will defend us?

TED: If everyone left isn't coolie, Kanaka or Japanese, then so am I.

CAMERON: Still, the government have given Zenski contract after contract for the railroads. Och, man, they aren't blind.

TED: If the government's not blind, then so am I.

DICK: The Russians will use Asiatics for the invasion and if that happens, none of us need hope for much quarter.

HEATHER: Asiatics!?

DICK: Asiatics!

TED: Asiatics!

DICK: Asiatics!

HEATHER: Oh, Dick!

EDITH: Heather, do you like my dress?

HEATHER: Oh, Edith—

CAMERON: Asiatics! You go too far, Dick!

NARRATOR: Does Dick go too far or not far enough?

Yes, Dick may be at rock bottom with nary a cent to his name, talking wildly of Asiatic invasion, but greater love hath no man than the passion he possesses for pale Heather Cameron.

DICK: Heather, I must have some action or I will rot.

I once read about the futility of seeking water-rich country in the heart of Western Australia. But in my gut I know it is there. I fancy I will venture to the Great Desert on instinct alone.

HEATHER: Water? Do you mean to try and find it, Dick?

DICK: I do. I will succeed on horseback where many camel expeditions have failed.

HEATHER: Dick, what if you never find water?

DICK: I will do my best.

HEATHER: You will die! Dick. You will die. I feel if I could have just given you another answer you would never have thought of this mad expedition. Am I right?

DICK: You are.

HEATHER: You know I love Philip Orloff. You promised to help me find him—and so you must know that my love is not mine to give. And besides that, how can you help me find him if you're looking for water?

DICK: Heather, for God's sake, don't let this phantom stand between us. Orloff can never come back to you: do you think that if he were alive he would have sent no message?

HEATHER: Mad, unreasonable as it may seem to you, Orloff holds me bound by ties which even the grave cannot break.

NARRATOR: Meanwhile, on a yacht off the coast, Count Zenski and Dromeroff make plans of attack.

ZENSKI: What news of General Leroy and his force of Mongol savages, *mon brave?*

DROMEROFF: Leroy and his fleet will be in the gulf by the end of the week.

ZENSKI: Excellent.

DROMEROFF: We will cut all communications. Except for those we send ourselves.

ZENSKI: And then we will land General Leroy and his army of Mongol savages in the middle of Queensland. There can be no mistakes.

NARRATOR: All the while, back at Isis Downs, Dick and Heather continue to debate his desire to find water in the West.

DICK: Heather, let me but have you here, and I will give you to him in the world beyond if it is your desire.

HEATHER: I cannot. Dick, you are too much of a man to ask me to betray both of us with a lie. I am not worthy of your love!

NARRATOR: What turmoil! What passion!

But there's no time to wallow in heartbreak as we follow the characters and the action up to Fort Mallarraway. Fort Mallarraway, the huge property run by Mr Musgrave. Musgrave is securing the property and talk soon turns to the threat of invasion.

CAMERON: What the deuce are you up to, Musgrave?

MUSGRAVE: I know you think I'm mad, Cameron. Foolish, even.

TED: Have you any idea when we may expect these infernal Russians?

MUSGRAVE: They may come any time. It can only be a question of weeks. Days even.

CAMERON: Days?

MUSGRAVE: Dick, could you collect a group of irregular horsemen to act as a mounted force? A cavalry even?

DICK: They'd need arms.

MUSGRAVE: Heavens to agony, if the government won't help us, we must help ourselves. Be self-sufficient, even.

CAMERON: I am with you. It may mean nothing—God send it does—but I will stand with you.

MUSGRAVE: Spoken like a man. A great man, even.

NARRATOR: And speaking of men speaking like men, a few days later, Zenski and Dromeroff are men speaking on a pier at Point Parker in Northern Queensland.

ZENSKI: With luck General Leroy should be here before the rise of the sun.

DROMEROFF: What is that light, *mon ami?* In the distance? Some fishermen?

ZENSKI: No. I think it is a messenger with the news direct from Leroy.

A MESSENGER *enters.*

MESSENGER: I am a messenger. I have come direct with news from Leroy.

DROMEROFF: *Pardieu!* General Leroy is on his way!

MESSENGER: The telegraph cables have all been cut.

I myself sent the last message from Noumea.

DROMEROFF: Noumea?

NARRATOR: Noumea.

MESSENGER: Noumea.

DROMEROFF: What did it say?

MESSENGER: War declared; be prepared for Russian attack on capitals.

DROMEROFF: War is declared!

ZENSKI: It begins! We are certainly ready to welcome *Monsieur le Général* and his army of the savage Mongols.

NARRATOR: And in the true tradition of a truly timeless classic, *The Yellow Wave* sheds light on the issues that continue to haunt contemporary Australia … boat arrivals.

Action sequence: Mongol horde arriving by sea (in a dragon boat).

NARRATOR: Thus, we meet the dynamic duo at the head of the Russian-Mongol force, Commissioner Wang and General Leroy. Leroy steps off the boat dressed in elaborate military attire. Wearing a black tunic cinched in at the waist and flared slightly at the hips with epaulettes on each shoulder, Leroy's boots have just hint of a cuff. However, it is Wang who turns heads in a long, yellow, silk coat bordered with real fur and a chain of priceless pearls. Thank you, Wang.

Bound by a common desire to conquer the Land Down Under, they are strange bedfellows—a Russian soldier of fortune and a sartorially elegant emissary of the great Chinese general, Ching Tu.

Then with a twist that would put Agatha Christie to shame, *The Yellow Wave* plays its trump card when it reveals the true identity of General Leroy. He is Orloff … Philip Orloff!

ZENSKI: Welcome home, Philip.

ORLOFF: Allow me to present to you my colleague, his Highness Commissioner Wang.

ZENSKI: Your Highness. May I say that is a lovely coat you are wearing. Is it genuine silk?

DROMEROFF: And those pearls, Your Highness. May I rub them on my teeth?

ZENSKI: Later.

ORLOFF: Round up the coolie dogs. I won't have any massacre of women; these men can be cruel when the lust of blood is on them! I will hang any man who takes part in such barbarity.

ZENSKI: *Mon brave*, are not all the men alike?

ORLOFF: Zenski, these are Mongols!

ZENSKI: Mongols!

DROMEROFF: Mongols!

ORLOFF: Mongols! No offence, Wang.

DROMEROFF: Come, Commissioner. You must be tired. Let me show you where you can rest your magnificent pearls.

DROMEROFF *ushers* WANG *out.*

ZENSKI: The bargain made on board ship all those years ago has been fulfilled at last, Philip. Victory is close. And when you win, the ball will be at your feet.

NARRATOR: World.

ZENSKI: The ball will be at your world.

ORLOFF: Where is Heather Cameron?

ZENSKI: At Isis Downs, but she and her father will soon seek the safety at Fort Mallarraway.

ORLOFF: Seek death, you mean! Zenski, why the devil didn't you send Heather and her father away?

ZENSKI: I am not her keeper. She will be well cared for. Rest easy.

ORLOFF: By God! Be careful, Zenski; remember, I love this woman.

ZENSKI: So does Dick Hatten.

ORLOFF: Who?

ZENSKI: Dick Hatten.

ORLOFF: Who?

ZENSKI: What?

ORLOFF: What?

ZENSKI: Dick Hatten.

ORLOFF: Huh?

NARRATOR: Dick Hatten.

ZENSKI: That's what I said … Dick Hatten. He was in your troop in Brisbane many years ago, I understand?

ORLOFF: Ah! Dick Hatten. Good-looking chap? About my height? Renaissance man? Good fellow, Dick Hatten.

So, Dick Hatten is my competition for Heather's love, is he?

ZENSKI: *Pardieu!* He would like to be, at any rate.

ORLOFF: Then, Heather does not love him?

ZENSKI: She has not made me her confidante. *Ma foi!* Why not let this woman marry whom she will, Philip? She is bad luck.

ORLOFF: I didn't ask your advice, Zenski.

ZENSKI: You were glad of it once, Philip.

ORLOFF: Sorry, Zenski. I haven't forgotten. It's just my will is not my own where Heather is concerned.

NARRATOR: Meanwhile, Dick Hatten is now the captain of the Northern Mounted Infantry. With weapons supplies scarce, Dick and his offsider Billy receive the worst possible news from Ted, recently returned from a scouting trip to Cloncurry.

DICK: Theodore!

TED: Dick, they've landed.

DICK: What—the Russians!

TED: No—the Chinamen!

DICK: Chinamen?

BILLY: Chinamen?

TED: Chinamen!

DICK: Where?

TED: Cloncurry. It's been given over to demons of blood and lust. They're everywhere.

DICK: My God! You don't mean that, Ted!

TED: By God, Dick, I do!

My horse broke down. I rode through the night. They're here I tell you. Pillaging, plundering, marauding …

DICK: We must stop them … we'll have to make our own lances.

TED: It'll take something to stop these demons.

BILLY: We'll tomahawk them, boss … like bloomin' ringers.

TED: It's the sound. It's like a devilish chorus.

DICK: You're a brick, old man! Go and have a sleep, Billy and I will make a start for town.

TED: Sleep be hanged! Wait while I have a drink of tea, and I'm with you.

BILLY: My oath, boss! There's a fresh pot made.

NARRATOR: But despite the men's boyish enthusiasm for lances, tomahawks and tea, Ted, fearing the impact of the Russian/Chinese soldiers on the women, makes the difficult but heroic decision to send Edith and her mother off to Sydney.

EDITH: Do take care of yourself, Ted. Everyone is looking forward to our wedding, I'd hate for you to get yourself killed and have to plan a funeral instead.

TED: Don't want you a widow before you're a proper wife. I won't let any man put their spear in me.

MRS ENSON: The way you young people talk!

EDITH *cries.*

TED: Don't cry, old girl. We'll clean up the Russians and the Chinamen. You'll see.

NARRATOR: And when the inevitable does happen in the form of marauding Mongols, *The Yellow Wave* takes us to the theatre of war, with battle sequences that leave nothing to the imagination.

Action sequence: 'Ave Maria'/machine-gun battle.

NARRATOR: Yes, war is hell and never more hellish than back at Fort Mallarraway where a council of war takes place and the men learn that Zenski's rail lines are blocked, making them completely impassable. One by one, the towns of Hughenden, Longreach and Townsville have fallen into Chinese hands. With the danger growing, and few options left for escape, Mr Musgrave tells the men they might have to make sacrifices … of the women.

MUSGRAVE: I consider it will be necessary to speak very plainly to the women, frankly even. In spite of our efforts, they may fall into the hands of these savages.

Every woman should carry a weapon. Have poison upon her person. That way, protection from worse than death may be assured.

If our women carry their fates in their hands, their husbands and brothers will fight with at least one weight of horror off their hearts. Off their shoulders, even.

NARRATOR: But some women, despite their sallow stoicism, are just too pale for martyrdom.

HEATHER: Dick, Mr Musgrave has told us that if the worst comes we must kill ourselves.

DICK: It won't come to that while I live.

HEATHER: I know that, you brave old fellow! But, Dick, I hate the thought of killing myself. I know it's weak, but I dread it; and so, when all is lost, if I must die, let it be by your hand.

DICK: You have asked much from me, Heather, this is more than I can do.

HEATHER: For the sake of the love your bear me, grant this last request. Your aim is sure, mine may fail, and then God help me.

DICK: If I am alive I will do what you ask.

NARRATOR: Life wasn't meant to be easy, Dick. Especially when your true love makes you promise to kill her in order to prove your devotion.

As if that isn't shocking enough, tragedy soon strikes at the heart of Fort Mallarraway as a large force of Mongol soldiers appears on the horizon.

DICK: By God, Ted … what's that on the horizon?

TED: Horsemen of some sort, Dick.

DICK: Mongols, Ted.

TED: Mongols, Dick.

What's that flag they're carrying?

DICK: I can't make it out.

TED: Dick, there is something about these Mongol savages that chills my blood. I hope you won't think less of me, old man.

NARRATOR: As if anybody could possibly think less of Ted. But the true horror of the scene takes on a nightmarish quality when the 'flag' the Mongol force is riding under is revealed to be a human head stuck on the point of a spear. It isn't long before horror after horror is rained down upon the fort.

Action sequence: Human head on a spear.

NARRATOR: In the midst of this we are shocked to learn of the demise of a man we have come to know little and admire slightly.

Action sequence: The death of Musgrave.

HEATHER: Oh, Dick, the destruction. The brutality! The horror! The annihilation! The despair!

Is something wrong, Dick?

DICK: Mr Musgrave is dead, Heather. I want you to tell his wife.

HEATHER: I will tell her, Dick.

DICK: Goodbye, Heather.

HEATHER: Goodbye, Dick.

NARRATOR: As Dick leaves to continue fighting the good fight, Heather is driven to take unexpected action with her attire.

HEATHER: Margaret, let us take off our dresses and put on trousers and coats. If we ride like the rest, we will have a better chance in every way.

MARGARET: If we've got to ride straddle-legs, get me a pair of trousers, Miss Heather, or it's rheumatics I'll be catching in my knees.

DICK *enters.*

HEATHER: Dick, I thought we just said goodbye. But since you're back … can you lend me a pair of trousers and a coat? I thought I would be less trouble to you with trousers on.

DICK: You're no trouble to me, Heather. Trousers on or off.

HEATHER: I like to do what I can.

DICK *takes her hand.*

DICK: Goodbye.

HEATHER: But I will see you again?

DICK: No.

HEATHER: To be fair, Dick, you've said that before.

DICK: Twice I have asked you for what you cannot give, girl! Let me hold you in my arms, kiss you on your lips, and I will weary you no more.

HEATHER: Oh, Dick.

DICK *stands with outstretched arms.* HEATHER *steps forward. They kiss passionately.* DICK *exits.*

NARRATOR: Fort Mallarraway is lost! As a last desperate resort, its residents scramble to escape the last of the marauding Mongol troops and their devilish destruction of life and limb.

Action sequence: Fort Mallarraway escape.

NARRATOR: Heather successfully escapes the carnage in her trousers. Dick, fired by his passionate interlude with Heather, blows up what is left of the fort and lives to fight another day.

Meanwhile, Heather runs straight from Dick's puckered lips into the threatening presence of a marauding Mongol officer.

ORLOFF: Halt!

KALMUCK SOLDIER 1: A man was attempting to escape, sir.

ORLOFF: Liar! It is a woman.

KALMUCK SOLDIER 1: I was saving her.

ORLOFF: Liar again! You have deserted your post to destroy her!

KALMUCK SOLDIER 1: Mercy!

ORLOFF *draws his revolver and shoots* KALMUCK SOLDIER 1.

HEATHER *loses consciousness and* ORLOFF *rests her head on his knee.* HEATHER *opens her eyes.*

ORLOFF: Heather! It's me, Philip Orloff.

HEATHER: Philip, you have come back at last. Oh, my darling! I have waited for you so long—so long!

NARRATOR: Haven't we all, Heather?

Yes, hot-tempered Philip Orloff is back in the arms of pale Heather Cameron … But, as she will soon discover … he's not all he seems!

HEATHER: Let's go, Philip, these wretches will see us and then even you will be powerless.

ORLOFF: You are knocked up, so I will put you on my horse.

Suddenly HEATHER *sees her father.*

HEATHER: Wait! Oh, Father! Father, you are not wounded! You are only tired! Philip, help me to lift him.

ORLOFF *bends down and places his arm under* CAMERON*'s head.*

CAMERON: I can't see you, dearie, but it's your voice. Who is with you, child?

HEATHER: It's Philip—Philip Orloff, Father. Philip?

CAMERON: Where? Who?

HEATHER: Philip Orloff. Philip, where are you—?

ORLOFF: Will you come with us, sir?

HEATHER: Philip has saved me, Father. Let us get you away before these murderers come back.

CAMERON: I am past all that, my darling Heather. Go before the savages murder you; Philip Orloff, I am going to give a charge into your hands. Heather has always loved you.

Promise me you will be to her what I would have tried to be.

ORLOFF *lays his hand on* HEATHER*'s shoulder.*

ORLOFF: Sir, I swear.

CAMERON: Your word is enough. Kiss me, child—I am going!

HEATHER *kisses* CAMERON. CAMERON *dies.*

HEATHER *and* ORLOFF *rise and another* KALMUCK SOLDIER *comes toward them.*

KALMUCK SOLDIER 2: *Pardon, Monsieur le Général.*

HEATHER: What have you to do with these men, Philip?

ORLOFF: I am not the man you once knew, and loved!

HEATHER: Not Philip Orloff? Then who are you, Philip?

ORLOFF: I am General Leroy. I am the leader of the Mongols.

Lifting her hands as if to ward off a blow, HEATHER *steps back.* ORLOFF *draws a revolver from his belt and offers it to her.*

Hate me, kill me, if you would do your country a service! But for God's sake! Don't look at me like that!

HEATHER *takes the revolver and raises it. She suddenly throws it to the ground.*

HEATHER: I dare not kill the man I love! Catch me, Philip.

HEATHER *falls to* ORLOFF*'s feet.*

NARRATOR: Yes, Philip Orloff is the leader of the Mongols. Just in case that wasn't clear.

Despite the gravity of this revelation, it is not the nature of *The Yellow Wave* to linger, and in no time three weeks have passed. Queensland is in a world of pain. Mongols are pouring in by the boatload. It seems that the Russian-led army has an unlimited supply of men. Ching Tu has taken Hong Kong and the British are in desperate straits in India. All looks hopeless as Queensland is held almost entirely by the Leroy-led Mongol force.

The night before yet another planned skirmish between the Australians and the Mongols, Count Zenski has some serious words for Orloff regarding the subjects of war, women and Wang.

ZENSKI: Remember, Philip, these Australians will not yield easily to an army of Chinamen. Even the well-dressed Chinamen.

ORLOFF: Their rabble will never get close enough to cross bayonets with my Mongols. I will sweep them away like flies.

ZENSKI: *Pardieu!* You and the good commissioner always remind me of that charming infant legend entitled 'The Monkey and the Nuts'.

ORLOFF: Well, this is the last nut I will pull out of the fire for the yellow hound!

ZENSKI: Careful, this Chinaman is ruthless. You risk giving the game into his hands—for a woman!

ORLOFF: For an angel.

ZENSKI: Bah! If you fall, a worse fate awaits her than the embrace of a Mongol savage.

ORLOFF: Zenski, what do you mean?

ZENSKI: Wang intends to keep her. For himself.

ORLOFF: The hound! After I have beaten the enemy, I will attend to His Highness Commissioner Wang.

NARRATOR: Yes, war may be hell, but it also provides a unique opportunity for advancement. Dick and Ted, now both officers, discuss another imminent battle with General Leroy and the Mongol army.

DICK: This battle is a mistake. We're throwing away our last chance.

TED: Surely we're too good for them man to man!

DICK: General Leroy is a clever beggar. My guess is he never intends to let us get close enough to find out.

NARRATOR: On the field of battle, Dick and his tomahawk-wielding troops do their best, but the Russian/Mongol army is formidable.

Action sequence: Hatten's Troops retreat.

NARRATOR: The Australian troops are comprehensively clobbered.

The cost is more than even Dick could have imagined as he wonders anxiously about the fate of an old friend.

DICK: No word, Billy? It's hopeless. I must try to get a message to Miss Edith and her mother. Somehow.

BILLY: How'll you break it to her? What'll you write?

DICK: Just … Ted's missing … presumed dead.

NARRATOR: Ted presumed dead! *The Yellow Wave* doesn't pull any punches. How uncanny of Edith to predict that she might be planning a funeral and not a wedding?

Some days later, on the battlefields of North Queensland, we find the strong, usually silent figure of Commissioner Wang inspecting the aftermath.

WANG: Our artillery has been more than effective, Mr Dromeroff.

DROMEROFF: Our success has exceeded all our hopes, Your Highness.

WANG: So it would seem. We will send word to Ching Tu immediately.

DROMEROFF: Tell me, is your coat handmade? Would you call the colour … canary yellow?

WANG *notices a leg quivering under a dead body. He gives it a kick.*

WANG: What was that? That leg moved.

DROMEROFF: *Pardieu*, Commissioner … these dead Australians are just like the proverbial chicken with its head cut off—

WANG: Nonsense, Dromeroff. That devil is still alive. Run your sword through him. Kill him. Kill him.

TED *suddenly rises up and makes straight for* WANG.

TED: Murder me, would you, you damned dirty Chinaman?!

TED *shoots his left fist into* WANG*'s face.*

DROMEROFF: Ted Johnson!

WANG: Kill him! Kill him!

ORLOFF *enters.*

ORLOFF: Hold! Take him prisoner. Then take His Highness Commissioner Wang to his carriage; his life, not to mention his coat, are too valuable to be risked among such scenes.

NARRATOR: Ted lives. He lives! As *The Yellow Wave* throws itself head first into its gripping denouement, Ted is now prisoner of the Russians and the Mongols.

Yet again, due to their profound urbanity, Zenski and Orloff are able to take a well-earned break to discuss this and other developments over a cigar and brandy.

ZENSKI: What will you do with Monsieur Ted Johnson?

ORLOFF: I promised that he would be removed from danger. I will keep my word.

ZENSKI: Bah! Let me guess who extracted that promise? The delightful Miss Cameron?

ORLOFF: I should let her go, Zenski. But it goes against all the desire of my being.

ZENSKI: You almost make me a believer in what you call 'love', Philip.

NARRATOR: In the end, Zenski is just a sentimental old count. But a little while later, Orloff and Heather's passionate relationship reaches a critical juncture.

HEATHER: Philip, you know that I will never love another, but we cannot go on as we are. Fugitive from everything decent.

ORLOFF: You ask me to give you your freedom?

HEATHER: Philip, we are not the same people we were on the *SS Genoa* all those years ago.

ORLOFF: Then I will set you free, my precious angel.

No matter that every fibre of my body fights against it.

HEATHER: Oh, Philip, my fibres fight it too!

NARRATOR: And thus, it is decided. Orloff and Heather join the pantheon of great star-crossed loves, Romeo and Juliet, Orpheus and Eurydice, Gillard and Rudd.

In order to secure Heather's safety, Orloff arranges for Heather and Ted to be spirited away to Sydney aboard a broken-down enemy cruiser, the *Hi Lung*. Up on deck, Zenski and Ted exchange pleasantries by way of farewell.

ZENSKI: *Bon voyage, mon ami!* Present my departing compliments to Mademoiselle Edith and her lovely mother.

TED: I'll see you to the devil first, you infernal cad!

ZENSKI: Till then *adieu, mon brave!*

NARRATOR: Not even direct insults ruffle Zenski's feathers.

Down below, though, Orloff is losing the battle with his fibres and is now having second thoughts about relinquishing his pale paramour.

HEATHER: Philip, you say you love me, and I know you do. For the sake of your love, will you do something for me?

ORLOFF: I will do anything but let you go.

HEATHER: I must go. But will you go, too?

ORLOFF: With you?

HEATHER: No. But will you?

Philip, for my sake, leave this life of murder and dishonour.

ORLOFF: No! But if you stay, I pledge myself that nothing you ask will be refused; for your sweet sake, I will change the face of Asiatic war.

HEATHER: —

ORLOFF: Be my wife, and you will be a queen! For you I will conquer both Australian and Mongol. Together we will found a new race of kings. A swarthy—

NARRATOR: —but pale—

ORLOFF: —hot-tempered—

NARRATOR: —but strangely passive—

ORLOFF: race of kings.

HEATHER: Philip, are you saying you won't let me go?

ORLOFF: Call me liar and a coward.

HEATHER: Are you saying you will let me go?

ORLOFF: I cannot let you go.

HEATHER: Are you saying you'll leave your ambition and power behind? Philip? I'm confused. What are you saying?

ORLOFF: I am saying I will go with you to the end of the earth!

HEATHER: Oh, Philip!

NARRATOR: And just as we think *The Yellow Wave* has given us the happy, joyous yet strangely ambiguous reunion we've been waiting for … the author produces another twist from up his impressive sleeve.

The Chinese fleet catches up to the *Hi Lung*, crashing into it and bringing about its almost total destruction.

Action sequence: The sinking of the Hi Lung.

NARRATOR: Amidst the chaos, Ted escapes, leaping aboard a nearby vessel to be either executed by the enemy or reunited with Edith and her mother. Neither of those options is without its shortcomings.

Within the sinking overturned wreck of the *Hi Lung*, Orloff finds Heather in a stateroom below deck. Together at last, but stranded on a sinking vessel, that for once isn't just a description of their relationship; they are trapped with less than five minutes of air between them.

ORLOFF: Heather, my love, speak to me.

HEATHER: Is that you, Philip? Are we there yet?

ORLOFF: My darling, we have but a few minutes of air left between us. I would strike myself dead if it would give you but one extra breath.

HEATHER: Philip, we are together at last. Let us live more in the moments we have left than we did in ten agonising years apart.

ORLOFF: When you say 'live'—

HEATHER: Oh, Philip, let us glory in our love for the rest of our mortal existence by forging a bond that will last for all eternity.

ORLOFF: When you say 'forging a bond'—

HEATHER: Nothing can come between us now, Philip.

ORLOFF: When you say 'nothing' …

HEATHER: We are safe at last. Safe where no Chinamen can lay spear or hand on us. … Our way of life, our values, my virtue … safe from Mongol savages. Safe from Chinese …

ORLOFF: When you say, 'safe' …?

Heather … my love … Heather … Heather.

NARRATOR: Side by side they died down in the depths of the sea. Oblivious to the wash of the waves that beat against their tomb and the restless winds that waft the good ships overhead. These two will lie at rest till the sea gives up her dead.

And so we bid a bittersweet *adieu* to the love story of Philip Orloff and Heather Cameron.

But what of the fates of Dick Hatten and Count Zenski? Will Ted marry Edith? Does Dromeroff ever find out if Commissioner Wang's pearls are real? And how long before the great General Ching Tu actually sets foot on Australian soil?

We will never know the answers to these and other questions. But this marvellous book and its kaleidoscope of characters have taken us on the richest of emotional voyages. So thrilling and moving that it hardly matters that *The Yellow Wave* is, in the end, a beautiful journey utterly devoid of a destination.

What a book! What an adventure!

THE END

THE YELLOW WAVE

JANE MILLER

From the novel by

Kenneth Mackay

10 – 21 May 2017

Director
Beng Oh

Set and Costume Designer
Emily Collett

Lighting Designer
Matthew Barber

Stage Manager
Daniel Barca

Performed by
Keith Brockett,
John Marc Desengano
and **Andrea McCannon**

CEO and Artistic Director
Liz Jones

Company Manager and Creative Producer
Caitlin Dullard

Marketing and Communications
Sophia Constantine

Design and Social Media
Jen Tran

Technical Manager
Hayley Fox

Front-of-House Manager
Amber Hart

Development Coordinator
Mary Helen Sassman

Office Coordinator
Elena Larkin

La Mama Learning Producer
Maureen Hartley

Preservation Coordinator
Fiona Wiseman

La Mama Musica Curator
Annabel Warmington

La Mama Poetica Curator
Amanda Anastasi

Script Appraiser
Graham Downey

La Mama Casting Service
Zac Kazepis

Intern
Mathilde Broudic

Level 1, 205 Faraday Street, Carlton VIC 3053
www.lamama.com.au | info@lamama.com.au
facebook.com/lamama.theatre | twitter.com/lamamatheatre
Office phone 03 9347 6948 | Office hours Mon–Fri, 10:30am–5:30pm

FRONT OF HOUSE

Susan Bamford-Caleo, Carmelina Di Guglielmo, Laurence Strangio, Dennis Coard, Darren Vizer, Robyn Clancy, and regular staff.

COMMITTEE OF MANAGEMENT

Sue Broadway, David Levin, Caroline Lee, Dur-é Dara, Peter Shaw, Kerry Noonan, Richard Watts and Liz Jones.

Our sincerest thanks to the many volunteers who generously give their time in support of La Mama.

La Mama's Committee of Management, staff and its wider theatrical community acknowledge that our theatre is on traditional Wurundjeri land.

The La Mama community acknowledges the considerable support it has received in the past decade from Jeanne Pratt AC and the Pratt Foundation.

La Mama is financially assisted by the Australian Government through the Australia Council – its arts funding and advisory body, the Victorian Government through Creative Victoria – Department of Premier and Cabinet, and the City of Melbourne through the Arts and Culture triennial funding program.

WRITER'S NOTE

Writing for theatre is, by its nature, collaborative. *The Yellow Wave* is the product of the collective effort of a group of artists over a long period of time. Kenneth Mackay's novel was originally identified by director Beng Oh who commenced exploring the potential for a theatrical adaptation with a group of actors that included Keith Brockett and John Marc Desengano. Their work included improvisation and devising, and it was some time later that I came on board to complete the adaptation process.

Aspects of Mackay's novel, written in 1895, are confronting when viewed through the prism of contemporary Australia. On one level, it is a classic romantic epic with a love triangle at its centre – not dissimilar to many literary blockbusters of yesteryear. However, the novel is also a unique artefact of its period and an Australian example of 'invasion fiction', a genre that reflects a fear of the 'foreign' or 'other'. In the context of this novel, the author is voicing anxiety about the imagined impact that he believes immigration and open borders might have on the social and cultural foundations on which the Australian society of the late 19th century perceived it had been founded.

While the book's narrative is written as a romantic adventure, in adapting it, we wanted to illuminate the issues it raises for discussion and for an audience to be able to draw their own parallels with those facing Australian society today. Cultural identity, stereotypes and border security are just two of the issues touched on in Mackay's narrative that are covered by contemporary media on a daily basis.

We deliberately chose comedy as the lens through which the adaptation should be viewed in order to engage and act as a starting point for in-depth conversations. We wanted it to be funny, but not trivial. Our challenge was to resist a temptation to overtly condemn or judge the attitudes expressed within the novel, as this would leave no room for an audience to make up its own mind and limit opportunity for further conversation.

It could be easy to dismiss the novel as paranoid or an example of propaganda, and a reading of this adapted play text in isolation might do little to persuade otherwise. However, to return to the original point, theatre is a collaborative art form and there is no question that as a theatre piece, the text and production of *The Yellow Wave* are inextricably linked. The framing of the production, as well as the cultural backgrounds and genders of the artists who created this piece, are as important to its overall dramaturgy, depth and layering as anything written on the page.

Jane Miller

Writer

Below: Andrea McCannon, Keith Brockett and John Marc Desengano. Photo by Lachlan Woods.

DIRECTOR'S NOTE

Published in 1895, *The Yellow Wave* is a heartfelt call-to-arms to defend Australia against ravening invaders who are hungry for our land, resources and women. It's a strident but sadly familiar call that, for all its absurdities, continues to resonate today.

We unearthed and adapted this classic novel with its patriotic, isolationist and xenophobic narrative as our contribution to the ongoing conversation about race, ethnicity, immigration, arrivals by sea, invasion and the presence of the 'other'.

We were also concerned about the lack of diversity in Australian theatre and its core myths of ability and plasticity, i.e. that non-white actors somehow simply aren't good enough and are only appropriate for a small selection of roles. So we set to work armed with two wonderful Asian Australian actors, Keith Brockett and John Marc Desengano, and were joined in time by our sharp-witted narrator, Andrea McCannon.

We crafted *The Yellow Wave* to challenge our performers and to showcase their multifarious skills and abilities. Its precision and pace, rapid changes and multiplicity of characters is testament to their talent. The

subversive humour, horseplay, silliness and absurdities that permeate the work comes from all of us. Combating fear has been a lot of fun.

Beng Oh
Director

Left: John Marc Desengano, Keith Brockett and Andrea McCannon. Below: John Marc Desengano and Keith Brockett. All photos by Lachlan Woods.

JANE MILLER
PLAYWRIGHT

Jane's work has been produced both in Australia and internationally. Her plays include *Perfect Stillness* (Short + Sweet), *The Painter* (MelBorn Melbourne Writers' Theatre), *Happily Ever After* (La Mama), the R.E. Ross Trust award winning *True Love Travels on a Gravel Road* (fortyfivedownstairs), *Motherf***er* (La Mama) and *Cuckoo* (fortyfivedownstairs). In 2013, Jane and director Beng Oh formalised their ongoing collaboration via the establishment of their company, 15 Minutes from Anywhere. In 2014 Jane completed a Master of Writing for Performance at the Victorian College of the Arts.

BENG OH
DIRECTOR

Beng is a Melbourne based Asian-Australian director who's staged a wide range of productions. He has directed plays by John Patrick Shanley, Paula Vogel, Peter Handke, Heiner Müller, Frank Wedekind, Gertrude Stein and Christopher Marlowe, among many others. He's passionate about diversity, new work and queer theatre and is attracted to heightened and non-naturalistic texts. Productions include George Tabori's farce *Mein Kampf*, *True Love Travels on a Gravel Road* by Jane Miller, the Australian premiere of *Tom Fool* by Franz Xaver Kroetz and *Porcelain* by Chay Yew. Beng completed postgraduate directing at the Victorian College of the Arts and is a member of the Lincoln Center Theater Directors Lab. He is co-artistic director of 15 Minutes from Anywhere and can usually be found in a rehearsal room somewhere.

EMILY COLLETT
SET AND COSTUME DESIGNER

Emily is a set and costume designer with a background in interior architectural design and dance, whose practice comprises theatre, dance, performance art, film, television and costume research. Her recent works include *The Yellow Wave* (La Mama), *Middletown* and *Eurydice* (Red Stitch), and *Dream Home* (Speak Easy at Northcote Town Hall), for which she was nominated for a 2016 Green Room Award for best set and costume design. Emily was the set and costume design candidate in MTC's Women in Theatre program in 2016 with mentor Christina Smith, and was accepted into the JUMP National Mentorship program in 2010 with mentor Hugh Colman. A move to London in 2011 saw Emily working for 18 months as Research Assistant to Donatella Barbieri, Senior Research Fellow in Design for Performance at the Victoria and Albert Museum. She has been assisting costume designer Marion Boyce since 2014 and is also currently a PhD candidate in Costume at VCA.

MATTHEW BARBER
LIGHTING DESIGNER

Matthew has designed and operated for productions in Melbourne over the past 25 years. Previous shows and collaborations with 15 Minutes From Anywhere and Beng Oh include: *The Hamletmachine* by Heiner Müller (Castlemaine State Festival); *Objects Lie On A Table* by Gertrude Stein, *Newtown Honey* by Marty Denniss, and *Motherf***er* (La Mama) and *Happily Ever After* (La Mama and on tour).

DANIEL BARCA
STAGE MANAGER

Daniel is a freelance lighting designer who has worked with a range of independent productions in Australia and the UK. He completed his Certificate IV in Live Production at NMIT's Fairfield campus in 2013. Daniel has worked with the likes of Tessa Waters, Backwards Anorak and Aunty Donna at Soho Theatre. His work includes festival tours of Edinburgh Fringe Festival (2014-15), Adelaide Fringe (2014-17), Melbourne International Comedy Festival (2014-17) and Melbourne Fringe (2013-15). Daniel was the Stage Manager and Lighting Designer/Operator for an original piece at La Mama, *Little Daughters*. Recently, Daniel has Stage Managed a range of shows also at La Mama including *Member*, *A Room of One's Own, Courage To Kill*, and *P.O.V. Dave*. This is Daniel's second season working with 15 Minutes From Anywhere and he looks forward to see what *The Yellow Wave* will bring.

KEITH BROCKETT
PERFORMER

Born in the UK, Keith Brockett trained at the National Theatre Drama School and the Royal Academy of Dramatic Art. Keith performs extensively in Australia, most notably for Melbourne Theatre Company, La Mama Theatre, 5Pound Theatre and 15 Minutes from Anywhere. He is also a founding member of The Kin Collective. Keith's film and television credits include: *The Librarians*, *Jack Irish*, *Rush*, *The Time of Our Lives*, *7 Types of Ambiguity*, *Warren and Hal*, and *Ronnie Chieng: International Student*.

JOHN DESENGANO
PERFORMER

Upon graduating from The University of Ballarat Arts Academy's acting course in 2008, John performed for theatre with education company Brainstorm Productions for five years. During this time he brought shows to high schools and primary schools all over Australia, tackling issues including bullying, substance abuse, and cultural diversity. In 2015 John completed a Masters of Primary Teaching at the University of Melbourne and now works as a casual relief teacher in various primary schools around the Greater Dandenong district. He has enjoyed working with director Beng Oh on *The Yellow Wave* since its first development in 2011 and credits the experience of the show and working with the creative team as being one that reinvigorated his passion for the performing arts.

ANDREA MCCANNON
PERFORMER

Andrea trained with The Actor's Company in London and The Rehearsal Room, 16th Street Actors Studio and Q44 Theatre in Melbourne. Local stage credits include *Requiem for the 20th Century* (Theatre@ Risk); *Anhedonia* (Fractured Femur Theatre); *Girls Do Gertrude* (Black Apple Theatre); *How I Learned to Drive*, *Quills* (Mockingbird Theatre); *Savage in Limbo* (Q44 Theatre); *Rosencrantz and Guildenstern Are Dead*, *Copenhagen*, *The Merchant of Venice*, *Dogg's Hamlet, Cahoot's Macbeth* (PMD Productions). On TV, Andrea's appearances include *Neighbours, Offspring, Miss Fisher's Murder Mysteries* and *Rush*.

STANDING OVATION FOR AUSTRALIA'S HOME OF INDEPENDENT THEATRE

In 2017, La Mama celebrates 50 years of nurturing new Australian theatre.

Built in 1883 for Anthony Reuben Ford, a Carlton printer, the building at 205 Faraday Street had been used as a workshop, a boot and shoe factory, an electrical engineering workshop and a silk underwear factory before becoming a theatre in 1967. La Mama was established by Betty Burstall and modelled on experimental theatre activities at La MaMa E.T.C., New York. Jack Hibberd's play *Three Old Friends* was the first play performed in the tiny space.

Since that time the crowded intimacy of La Mama has provided welcome opportunities to a host of playwrights, actors, directors, technicians, film-makers, poets and comedians, such as David Williamson, Barry Dickins, John Romeril, Tes Lyssiotis, Lloyd Jones, Arthur and Corinne Cantrill, Judith Lucy, Richard Frankland, Julia Zemiro, and Cate Blanchett ... the list of those who have been nurtured there is long.

Under the capable care of Liz Jones (Artistic Director since 1976), and her La Mama team, more than 50 productions are now produced annually at La Mama, and at our second performance venue, the refurbished La Mama Courthouse, 349 Drummond Street. An ever-increasing audience is drawn not only from the Carlton and Melbourne University environs, but from far and wide across the country.

'I set La Mama up, as a space for writers and directors to perform in but also it was a space where people came, as audience, to participate in the creative experiment.'

—Betty Burstall, Artistic Director of La Mama 1967–76

'Much will be said of La Mama's role in developing a new generation of Australian writing. However, in considering policies and personalities, one should not forget the nature of the space and its impact in making possible performances that would be lost in a large theatre. It gave performances the intimacy of the cinema close-up with the exciting immediacy of the live theatre and the warmth of the coffee lounge.'

—Daryl Wilkinson, Director

La Mama Theatre—which, on various occasions, has been called headquarters, the source, the shopfront and the birthplace of Australian theatre—was classified by the National Trust in 1999.

'The two story brick building is of State cultural significance because it has been occupied by La Mama Theatre... The building is indelibly associated with the performance arts and is a rare manifestation of an experimental theatre in Australia...'

—National Trust Classification Report

When it comes to grassroots Melbourne theatre, La Mama in Carlton is like the 60GB iPod—small, subtle, but containing a whole lot more than you might expect.

—John Bailey, *Age*

La Mama produces work from two venues: 205 Faraday Street, Carlton (opposite top), and at the La Mama Courthouse, 349 Drummond Street, Carlton.

For current La Mama productions and events, see www.lamama.com.au.